Gaudí and the Mystique of Nature

Antoni Gaudí y Cornet (1852-1926) was born half way through the nineteenth century into troubled Spanish times. His fellow countryman and contemporary Mariano Fortuny was a correspondent during the African war of 1860, one of the great historical events of the period, which broke out in Morocco and lasted until 1925, the year before Gaudí's death.

Seventeen years before the artist was born, in 1835, the suppression of religious assets was ordered, the property of religious orders confiscated and monks massacred throughout Spain.

In Catalonia, as well, Gaudí's own lifetime saw the three "Carlist" civil wars waged between followers of Queen Isabella II and those of her uncle, Don Carlos. Gaudí also lived through the period of anarchy in Barcelona, marked by the bombing of the Lyceum Theatre in the city in 1897, and the tragic week-long revolution of July 1909, when many Barcelona churches and convents were burnt.

His life story is indeed set in times of upheaval. Born in the reign of Isabella II, he lived through the reign of Amadeus I of Savoy, the First Republic, the Restoration of Alfonso XII and most of the reign of Alfonso XIII, which began with the regency of Queen Maria Cristina and ended with the military dictatorship of General Primo de Rivera.

At the time of Gaudí's birth, French Classicism was the dominant influence on the Spanish cultural and artistic scene. Shortly after, the troubadour style, with its paintings on historical themes, became popular together with romantic decoration. Architecture was heading towards the eclecticism that the masters of Mo-

dernism attempted to wipe out at the end of the century.

In order to understand the greatness of Gaudí, we need only study his work. Despite its great uniqueness and independence from contemporary trends, however, the work of this great master does not make full sense unless examined in the light of his artistic surroundings and Barcelona's position of prominence in Spanish art. Although Gaudí was born in the Tarragona countryside and made much of his birthplace, most of his work can be found in Barcelona, a city he abandoned few times in his life and even then only for short periods.

His trips abroad included only a short excursion to the South of France when a student and another similarly brief jaunt to Tangiers in Morocco in 1892. Within Spain he sometimes spent time in Astorga, where he built the Bishop's Palace, and in Leon, where he built the Casa de Los Botines. Barcelona is therefore the natural environment for Gaudí's work – and its best backdrop.

Although traced back to the legends of Hercules, we really have to thank the Romans for giving us Barcelona. The city acquired a certain importance during the first century, when it was known as *Faventia Pia Augusta Paterna Barcino*. The Empire has left some archaeological remains, such as the Temple of Augustus and in particular the early city wall built at the beginning of the fourth century. Despite the fact that this lay hidden for centuries under later constructions, it nevertheless played a key rôle in determining the layout of the city's historical centre.

The late Middle Ages left behind a few faint traces in Barcelona, passed down by the Visigothic kings and Muslim domination, and a few hints remain of the time when the city was governed by counts who either acted as feudal overlords for the Frankish king or ruled independently.

Certain noteworthy monuments in the city date from Roman times, such as the Bishop's Palace, the Cathedral, S María de Las Arenas and the S Pablo del Campo monastery — though none of these have earned much mention in architectural history books.

The Gothic period was much more important and decisive, particularly the fourteenth century when Barcelona enjoyed its heyday in the Mediterranean, and Corsica, Sardinia, Sicily and part of mainland Greece were all part of the kingdom of Aragon. Architecture flourished in the city at this time and found original forms of expression. Indeed, within the space of little more than a century, churches such as the Gothic cathedral, S Justus and the Holy Shepherd, S María del Mar, the Pino, the monasteries of Pedralbes, Montesion and Junqueras, the Town Hall — and a great number of buildings and private houses — were built.

Catalan Gothic art is highly imaginative with a distinctive style of its own that greatly influenced Gaudí. He was able to study these Gothic monuments and then consult the theories of Viollet-le-Duc to find out more about the principle that lay behind their structural design. This point is crucial to our understanding of some of Gaudí's distinctive forms since he did not base his work, like many of his contemporaries, on the Neogothic style of Viollet, Pugin, Scott, Street, Gau, Boisserrée or Brentano.

Gothic art in Catalonia is actually more closely related to Roman design than to the *opus francigenum* of northern Europe. Gothic naves are exceptionally wide in Catalonia; for example, the nave of Gerona Cathedral measures almost 23 metres in width. Medieval Catalan architects cared more about width than height and above all about the lightness and "transparency" of an interior. This is particularly evident in three cases, namely S María del Mar in Barcelona, S María del Aurora in Manresa and the Cathedral of Palma in Mallorca. All are built with delicate, slender octagonal columns and on a square rather than triangular plan. A famous discussion took place between Italian and French engineers in Milan in 1391, over whether to use the "ad quadratum" or "ad triangulum" system in the construction of the Duomo. In S María del Mar (1328-1383) the bays of the main nave are perfectly square and the vaults overhead are therefore crossed in Roman style with delicate Gothic ribbing that is purely decorative.

This insistence on Latin basilica proportions was at odds with the verticalism and elaborate decoration typical of French, English and German Gothic styles and peculiar to medieval Catalan architecture. This trend was also adopted by Gaudí, who considered himself closely related to the Latins and Greeks and distanced himself from Anglo-Saxon and German sensibilities — despite his Franco-German family origins.

After a glittering fourteenth century, the late

Gothic period of the fifteenth and an early flowering of the Renaissance, Barcelona slumped into a long period of cultural lethargy. This happened because Catalonia went into a decline as a result of its union with Castille and because Spanish activities in the Americas and the Atlantic relegated the Mediterranean to second place. Many Renaissance buildings in Barcelona feature an odd blend of the new style and the predominating Gothic. Even as late as the mid-seventeenth century, churches were still being built with Gothic groin vaults but classical façades.

Non monumental buildings were erected during the Baroque period but this was the age of master sculptors who specialised in the creation of complex, scenic, gilt altar-pieces, installed in the chapels of Gothic churches. Gaudí's interest in Baroque altar-pieces is worth a mention. In the Sanctuary of Mercy at Reus, the Chapel of the Virgin, destroyed in 1936, contained a piece by the Baroque sculptor Bonifàs that Gaudí liked very much. He saw in its style an expression of vitality, an expressive force that interested him, not so much in terms of sculpture for its own sake, but as a possible source of inspiration for new architectural forms. When he was summoned to Manresa in 1916 to discuss the planned restoration of the Gothic cathedral's façade, he was really more interested in the Baroque altar-pieces than the equally valuable Gothic paintings kept in the cathedral. On one occasion he even said that if commissioned to design a work in Madrid he would base it on the Baroque forms of Ribera.

At the end of the eighteenth century and during the first few years of the nineteenth, Barcelona was more influenced by French Classicism than the Imperial style. The most important building of this peroid, the marketplace Loggia, was built by applying the architectural forms of Gabriel or Mansart to an ancient Gothic building. This fortunately retained intact its large gallery with a trussed roof on central pillars − a solution frequent in Catalan Gothic architecture. Neoclassical style never really took off in Barcelona since the city suffered the consequences of the Napoleonic occupation and came out of it much the worse for wear.

When Gaudí arrived in Barcelona in 1869, aged seventeen, he discovered an architectural panorama rich in ancient monuments and lacking in contemporary works but with great promise for the future. The Catalan Modernist style developed during this period. This had three main points of departure we would do well to consider. In the first place, the walls that circled the city were knocked down in 1859. All the buildings and inhabitants were crammed into a very restricted space until that date. On the other side of the wall and citadel extended a large, flat area, well positioned and protected from cold winds by the coastal cordillera. This contained no buildings because it had always been a military zone. The same year, 1859, saw the approval of a plan by the engineer and town planning expert Idelfonso Cerdà. The plan was based on the simple town planning principles of Ippodamo and offered the opportunity of building a completely new city. Unfortunately, taking down the wall proved to be a serious blunder since this structure originally marked the edge of ditches and slopes constituting a green belt for the city. The necessary extension to the city could have been carried out without getting rid of the wall and ditches — as was achieved in the Tuscan town of Lucca. For political and economic reasons this was not done and the land formerly occupied by the wall has been entirely built up, with the result that the city now includes very few green areas.

The way now lay open for the new city, but two factors in particular were responsible for turning the dream into reality. The first of these was the setting up of the Barcelona Provincial School of Architecture with the principal aim of training the engineers who were to construct the new buildings. Previously, from 1850 to 1870, there had existed only the School of Master Builders. Prior to that, the Corporation of Builders had been turning out excellent artisans since the thirteenth century who were, nevertheless, completely ignorant of up-to-date engineering techniques and lacked any academic training.

The other important factor that made it possible to build a new city was the prosperity that came from Barcelona's flourishing textile and mechanical engineering industries and the thriving trade with America, particularly the island of Cuba, which began to develop during the time of Carlos III when the Mediterranean ports were banned from trading with America.

Given the presence of an area suitable for development, a master plan and young architects trained at a local school, it is hardly surprising that Barcelona underwent a building boom.

The first timid, faltering steps towards building the new city were taken around 1870, at first by architects of the eclectic school, trained at the S Fernando Academy in Madrid, or humble master builders — really second-rate architects who had only studied for three years — but later by a new generation of architects from the Provincial School who threw themselves into their task with missionary zeal.

Interestingly engough, the first head of the Barcelona Provincial School of Architecture was Don Elías Rogent Amat, an enthusiastic Medieval scholar who extolled the virtues of Medieval Catalan architecture to his pupils and encouraged them to go out and see things for themselves, an adventurous undertaking given the almost complete lack of main roads. Students with an interest in ancient Roman and Gothic monuments probably benefited far more from this first-hand experience than from reading text books. Rogent was true to his own teachings when he built the new university and seminary in a blend of Gothic and Renaissance styles, inspired by civil architecture of the fifteenth and sixteenth centuries.

The first architects to graduate from the Barcelona school therefore emerged into an auspicious environment. Only three managed to qualify in the first year of 1872. A few years later, another event took place that was to prove extremely important in the future architectural rebirth — the Universal Exhibition of 1888. This meant that now, twenty years after the land had been designated for the expansion of Barcelona and a little more than ten years after the setting up of the School of Architecture, the forty-four graduates had the chance to build spectacular, imposing buildings worthy of a great international exhibition. Acting on the orders of the now elderly Rogent, all the architects in Barcelona contributed to the buildings in the Exhibition, which was built in the park on the site of the old citadel in 1873.

Catalan Modernism

Some writers such as José Francisco Ráfols maintain that the 1888 Exhibition marked the beginning of Catalan Modernism. Since 1875, architecture in Barcelona had been undergoing a change in direction due to the influence of Josep Vilaseca and Lluís Domènech who embarked on a long journey throughout Europe in 1872 and imported a fashion for the German style which became popular after the Franco-Prussian war. This was joined by another known as *neo-mudéjar* that grew up in Madrid but quickly took root in Barcelona. Certain characteristics of this style were later considered peculiar to Spanish architecture, such as the use of bare brickwork and horseshoe arches. The first works by Domènech and Vilaseca displayed these features. These included the headquarters of the Montaner and Simon publishing company built by Lluís Domènech and Montaner and the triumphal archway of the 1888 Exhibition, designed by Josep Vilaseca.

This combination of circumstances provided fertile ground for the growth of Catalan Modernism, a movement that was to pave the way for the rest of Europe. The Catalan movement was preceded only by William Morris's English Arts and Crafts Movement, based on the theories of John Ruskin. Between 1888 and 1893, the construction date of Victor Horta's Hotel Tassel in Brussels, considered the first Art Nouveau work, numerous buildings in Barcelona were constructed in the distinctive style that later spread throughout Europe under the name of Jugendstil, Secession, Liberty and so on.

It is significant that Modernism is considered the second great style in Barcelona after Gothic. Only in the fourteenth century and the decades that straddled the nineteenth and twentieth centuries did Barcelona display such a pronounced and distinctive artistic and architectural personality. Many houses in Barcelona are built in the Modernist style and many major architects participated in the movement. In addition to Vilaseca and Domènech, other figures of equal stature were Enric Sagnier, Pere Falqués, Salvador Viñals, Antoni Gallissà, Josep Puig y Cadafalch and many others.

Josep Vilaseca y Casanovas (1848-1910) was, just like a Renaissance Humanist, an all-embracing Modernist who worked not only as an architect but also as a decorator, designer, painter and even actor. His friend and colleague Lluís Domènech y Montaner (1850-1923) was the key figure of the Modernist movement. He was also a multi-talented genius involved in politics, archaeology, heraldry and art history with enough time left over to be an excellent designer and watercolour artist. As an architect, he restored monuments in the romantic style of Viollet-le-Duc but with a more lively imagination – as, for example, in the castle of Santa Florentina at Canet de Mar where the Neogothic design is complemented by totally idiosyncratic details. An interesting design for the completion of the Gothic lantern at the Poblet Monastery was drawn up but never executed.

On of the most remarkable and important designs was for the S Pablo Hospital in Barcelona, which consists of numerous pavilions joined by underground passages. This outstanding example of avant-garde hospital architecture features the brillant forms and rich colours of the Modernist style. Another glorious example of the same style is Barcelona's Palacio de la Musica, a concert hall owned by Orfeó Català that combines all the distinctive features of Modernism: multi-coloured mosaics, tiles decorated with motifs and relief patterns designed by the architect, stained glass, sumptuous lamps of metal and glass, huge mock stone sculptures painted white and absorbed within the architectural structure – one example is the colossal Flight of the Valkyries which forms the proscenium of the concert hall (1905-1908).

After Domènech, we should also give equal space to the personality of Josep Puig y Cadafalch (1867-1956), a doctor of mathematics, archaeologist, architect, student of Roman architecture, writer and researcher who, from 1897 onwards, completed an impressive array of works. In these he combined a late Gothic style with *mudéjar* and Plateresque to produce an extremely picturesque and imaginative blend of architectural styles. In the wake of Catalan Modernism, he joined architects of the next generation embracing the Viennese models offered by Olbrich and Wagner, and the Germans Poelzig and Behrens. The twentieth century then marked a return to classical, Mediterranean forms inspired by folk tradition, in turn overtaken by the impact of European Rationalism in the Thirties. This then was the architectural and artistic climate in Barcelona during the period when Gaudí worked in the city.

Because Gaudí was active at this extremely fertile time, he is often considered a leading light within the same movement, in other words, one of the Catalan Modernist architects. However, a more detailed examination of his work reveals this generalisation to be unfounded. Gaudí stands alone not only in terms of his relationship with the Modernist movement but also with all other earlier or contemporary styles. At the beginning of his career his style displays certain elements of Islamic architecture – and Gothic influences creep in at all stages. These are always marginal to his work, though, and completely "reabsorbed" into his architecture. This seems a good point to examine his personal style and identify the ways in which it differs from that of his fellow countrymen and contemporaries.

Inspiration from nature

Gaudí was an architect first and foremost – and never pretended to be anything else. He did not care about writing and being published: only two of his articles were printed, one in 1881 and the other in 1916. He never wished to teach or lecture in any conventional sense and was content with showing illustrious visitors round his

Church of the Sagrada Familia. He never played any part in politics and turned down unequivocally the chance to become an MP. He lived alone and therefore never experienced marriage or family life.

His passion was for the art of architecture in the widest sense of the word. He even considered it a sort of religion, just as he saw religion in the same light as architecture since it too was harmonious, ordered work carried out by the Creator.

This lack of interest in anything that was not strictly architectural was reflected in his way of seeing the world. Gaudí was a perceptive and avid observer of nature and had been fascinated since he was a boy by the structural solutions provided by animals, plants and rocks.

He had a heightened decorative sense and appreciated the way nature manages to resolve complicated structural problems while still adopting the form most pleasing to the eye.

In his architectural work he realised he had to find solutions that resolved the problems of balance and aesthetics at one stroke. He was certainly convinced that however many experiments he made, he could never hope to match the number carried out by nature at the first moment of creation.

He designed branching pillars for the Sagrada Familia in the conviction that the structure of a tree is uniquely perfect, has been tried and tested through the ages and needs neither additions nor refinement. It took Gaudí to apply this sort of logic, in other words a keen observer with a mind unfettered by any intellectual prejudices.

The Modernist movement of Gaudí's day also made abundant use of floral motifs in the decoration of tiles, windows, stucco and paintings. But Modernist flowers were never true to nature. They underwent a process of intellectual transformation and were simplified, forced into artificial symmetry or asymmetry in such a way that the overall aesthetic effect was pleasing but not absolutely true to nature. Gaudí could not have worked in this way. His observations of plants and animals provided him with ideal concepts for building architectural structures — we know of no structure more advanced than a vertebrate's skeleton — while at the same time offering him inspiration for colours, textures and patterns that he knew he could not better. It was sufficient for him to copy the flowers, birds and snakes exactly as they were. The quantity and complexity of forms and models in nature was so enormous that it was logical for Gaudí to develop a way of simplifying and rationalising the huge amount of information that offered itself to his probing mind. This need led him to develop and use a new type of geometry for the design of architectural forms — a type new to architecture but not to nature.

Since the time of the Egyptians and Ancient Greeks, architects have always given precedence to the use of straight lines and two- or three-dimensional geometrical shapes. Architectural designs throughout the ages have always relied on the use of a ruler and compass together with slide-rule and set-square. These implements can be used to draw triangles, squares, circles and rectangles that can be arranged to produce a three-dimensional figure also elementary in character, namely a sphere, cube, prism or pyramid.

Gaudí saw that these forms do occur in nature but only very rarely. And when theq to they are always objects of curiosity: cubes of pyrites and dodecahedrons of cinnabar fill glass cases in natural history museums together with other mineral prisms and pyramids.

These empirical forms have been considered a representation of the original elements of creation since ancient times. In *Timeus,* Plato likened the tetrahedron to air, the icosahedron to water and the cube to earth. A pentagonal dodecahedron was considered the quintessential form and, together with the sphere, the geometrical body most laden with symbolism.

But symbolism and simplified abstraction played no decisive part in Gaudí's thoughts on architecture. He took his work from nature because nature is tangible reality, balance and aesthetics all in one.

The Parabolic Arch, Hyperbolic Paraboloid and Helicoid

From the very beginning of his career, Gaudí made use of the parabolic arch − considered the most rational and "mechanical" of all arches. Architects have used this form only rarely throughout the ages − the Ctesiphon palace included parabolic arches designed by Byzantine architects − since it is more difficult to construct than a round or pointed arch.

The carpenters who prepare arch frames also find a round or even elliptical arch easier than a parabolic arch. In Sierra de Prades, above Reus, where Antoni Gaudí spent his childhood, a natural arch has been weathered out of the mountain by the wind. Its outline is perfectly parabolic. With all the logic of childhood, Gaudí must certainly have thought that if nature made arches in that shape it must surely have been for reasons of simplicity and practicality.

Ehen he came to study in the Barcelona School of Architecture, he most probably came across scientific books by Rondelet or Millington in the library describing the parabolic arch as the most ingenious of all arches. They called it a "balanced arch" because it follows the pressure lines − and also added that, due to its unpleasant shape, it was hardly ever used. Gaudí rejected this aesthetic prejudice out of hand since he believed its beauty lay in its functionality. Gradually, as his architectural beliefs began to take shape, he studied other geometrical shapes that were as simple as empirical geometrical solids yet at the same time different and more closely related to forms occurring in nature.

From then on, Gaudí's architecture was based quite definitely on the hyperboloid, hyperbolic paraboloid and helicoid: curves made up entirely of straight lines. The hyperbolic parabolid is the curved surface described by the movement of a straight line known as the generatrix that moves in turn over two other lines not parallel in space known as directrices. The result is a saddle shape that extends to infinity.

The shape of a femur is, on the other hand, very similar to that of a hyperboloid. Each human hand contains four hyperbolic paraboloids if we consider the fingers, two by two, as directrices and the tendons joining them as generatrices. When a tree is felled, we can see that its trunk grows according to a helicoid pattern. Gaudí's watchful eye allowed him to perceive the geometry hidden in animals and plants — and apply it successfully to his buildings to achieve balanced, appealing forms similar to those produced by nature through millions of years of evolution.

In the portico to the crypt of the Güell estate he used vaults and walls based on hyperbolic paraboloids for the first time in the history of architecture and more than half a century before the Organicist architects attempted to do the same thing.

The vaults in the Sagrada Familia were designed in hyperboloid form because of the ease with which the frames could be prepared and because the paraboloid is the ideal shape for letting sunlight into an enclosed space. For these reasons, Gaudí's constructions were based on a geometry different from that used by most architects.

The basic idea of using nature as a model was supplemented by decorative systems that were exact copies of patterns appearing in zoology, geology and botany. The results were surprising. At first glance, Gaudí's exuberant façades bring to mind the dynamism and wealth of ornamentation typical of Art Nouveau, even though the starting points and final outcomes are actually quite different.

No-one who has examined in detail the façade of Casa Milà in Barcelona, supposed to represent an underwater reef, could imagine they were looking at an example of Art Nouveau or Jugenstil.

The essence of Gaudí's architecture is timeless and its skilled yet fantastic system of construction could equally well have come from a Gothic master as from most avant-garde of present-day architects. Unlike the Modernist movement, now a closed chapter, having sprung from a brief outburst of Catalan euphoria, the complex yet simple architectural ideas of Gaudí remained essentially unchanged — though they developed as their author gained experience and lived through the many different architectural trends of the period: from Eclecticism to Modernism, Rationalism, Expressionism and Organicism. Only a certain number of the members of these movements, such as Sullivan and Wright, appreciated the importance of Gaudí's towering, isolated figure. He was engaged in the creation of a new architectural language designed not so much to provide a new means of expression but to reveal a new concept of architecture, which saw this art form as a continuation of the Creator's work and therefore steeped in Christian religious significance.

All Gaudí's buildings incorporate religious symbols whether or not they were designed as churches or convents. A rough-hewn cross occupies the highest point of Casa Batlló, Bellesguard, Parque Güell and Casa Milà. The Palacio Güell also culminates in a cross and the same was planned for Chalet Graner and Casa Miralles.

With its Catholic and therefore Latin roots, this profound religious sentiment is a blend of eastern spiritualism and pagan symbolism that

Gaudí upheld with an utter disregard for all the intellectual artistic tendencies of his time. He cut himself off so completely that he spent the last few years of his life shut away in the ivory tower of his Sagrada Familia, far from the fashions, crises and struggle for fame and recognition usually so common among artists.

Gaudí has been compared to the Medieval masters, and attempts have been made to link his work with the ancient, picturesque world of cabbalistic images and alchemy. This comparison bears scrutiny in only one respect: Gaudí, like the architects who built the great cathedrals of the thirteenth and fourteenth centuries, wanted to produce a work that was perfect in every respect. Just as the ancient Gothic master glaziers made authentic grisaille miniatures to be positioned twenty or thirty metres up where no-one would ever see them, Gaudí paid great attention to perfecting even the tiniest details of his architecture, however inaccessible the position, ever true to his belief that buildings are art and art is a human reflection of divine glory.

A study of the symbols used in the design for the Sagrada Familia reveals Gaudí's ingenuity in combining a large amount of information relating to the liturgy and worship. If we look at the Parque Güell from this point of view, we discover obvious religious imagery in the gardens and naturally occurring spaces, which reveals Gaudí's dual objective: to select certain motifs from nature and change them into religious symbols, or to seal the religious imagery within nature and place the two elements in close contact, so linking them for eternity.

We could envisage Gaudí as an architect inspired by the same love of nature as St Francis of Assisi, with whom he also shared an awareness of poverty, since many of Gaudí's works use discarded material such as brocken glass, pieces of majolica ware and tile fragments in an attempt to show that the final appearance of an architectural work is independent of the intrinsic quality of the material used.

As for the repercussions of Gaudí's architecture today or in the future, an attempt to create a Gaudiesque image by imitation or by copying buildings designed by the great architect would be inappropriate. There is no doubt, however, that we could use his innovative geometrical ideas to generate a new architectural language, if the purpose of this were to imitate his direct and constant relationship with nature. This approach could offer a whole range of solutions to the problems of present-day architecture and town planning.

The word ecology was not yet in use when Gaudí was alive, although he was certainly the first ecological architect, since his buildings blend in perfectly with the natural environment from which they take their form. In the case of Parque Güell, it is difficult to distinguish the works of nature from those designed by Gaudí.

One characteristic of the architect was his indifference to official rules and regulations, and a certain wariness with regard to mathematical calculations — however useful — which he considered excessively abstract and therefore dangerous. Gaudí preferred his very simple but extremely accurate system of empirical calculation to the complications of advanced mathematics. In this too, Gaudí was ahead of his time since some present-day architects believe that computers are threatening to dehumanise architecture and town planing.

One should point out that Gaudí did not reject the application of mathematics per se, but wanted to keep it within reasonable limits to prevent such calculations from prevailing over man's intelligence and will. Gaudí also considered architecture to be the highest form of fine art and maintained that any architectural element demanded artistic ability. He believed that the result was always an object of monumental character, which is another way of saying that architecture must be monumental or it is not architecture. In some cases it would be safer to call it civil engineering.

As he was strolling down the Paseo de Gracia in Barcelona one day with his pupil Juan Bergos, they passed the Casa Mila and Gaudí said: "When I built this house, I was helped by two brothers. One was an ordinary building contractor and the other an architect, a lecturer in structure. The former was more use to me than the latter".

Gaudí's personality, so different from that of most architects, was very Iberian in its rebelliousness, sense of dignity and pride without arrogance.

In this sense he is a faithful reflection — the quintessential Platonic "pentagonal dodecahedron" — of his native land, drenched in light with its stark forms, colours, craggy mountains, stony plains and coasts lapped by the blue Mediterranean — master of his art and voice of the Graeco-Latin culture.

*Fountain on a stairway in Parque Güell incorporating the
Shield of Catalonia and serpent's head.*

Casa Vicens

Isolated within the panorama of modern architecture, yet
without doubt one of its most prominent figures, Antoni
Gaudí gave his imagination free rein when designing his
buildings. Although an accomplished engineer, he used this
ability only as a tool to achieve increasing freedom and
boldness. In his work structure and function take second place
after form. This is underlined in the way a variety of materials
and decorative features are combined in an expressive
interplay that envelops the whole construction. The vivid
colour combinations are taken from nature. Gaudí was active
mainly in Barcelona because local patrons were particularly
open to new influences, and artisans in the Catalan capital
were particularly skilled in the use of his favourite materials:
wrought iron, terracotta, ceramics, glass and stone. Gaudí
used these materials almost in the same way as a sculptor,
continually altering the formal definition of the whole and its
parts. His first major work was Casa Vincens, designed in
1883 for Manuel Vincens Montaner, a relatively unknown
manufacturer of ceramics and bricks, within the ancient Villa
de Gracia, which became part of Barcelona in 1897. The
building was extended and refurbished in 1925 by the architect
Joan Baptista de Serra de Martínez with Gaudí's permission. It
is still a private house and retains its original furnishing and
many of the decorative features. The exterior is characterised
by projecting structures and is built in bare brick. It is covered
with glazed ceramic tiles with wild flowers and sunflowers in
relief alternating with plain green and white tiles. The theme is
reminiscent of Muslim architecture, familiar to Gaudí from
photographs in the library of the School of Architecture. Casa
Vicens consists of a basement with cellars and utility rooms, a
main floor with dining room, an adjoining gallery with small
fumoir, and a top floor with bedrooms. The particularly
interesting exterior ironwork features palm leaf motifs typical
of Gaudí. Facing page, the main entrance to Casa Vicens.

16

The interior of Casa Vicens displays a relatively traditional room layout. The rich decoration is based on an eclectic range of sources, freely reinterpreted. Gaudí designed the decoration in the dining room (shown on these pages) down to the very last detail, including walls and ceiling. The ornate walls are decorated with a graffito design of green ivy shoots on a gilt background interspersed with fine paintings by José Torrescassana Pallarés (1845-1918), a pupil of Ramón Martí Alsina.

The fireplace (below), positioned between two doors leading into the gallery, features a fine surround of tiles with floral motifs. The insides of the door frames consist of panels painted with exotic birds in contemporary English style. The floor mosaic, furniture with original locks and picture frames are all designed by the Catalan architect. Gaudí's furniture made an important contribution to the history of furnishing in introducing new concepts which transcended the limits of pure ornamentation.

In the dining room of Casa Vicens, the wooden beams (shown here) are laid on brightly coloured trusses. The exhuberant multi-coloured decoration between the beams represents leaves, berries and shells. The ceiling of the gallery adjacent to the dining room consists of vaults and domes painted to resemble an open roof covered with large palm trees. The gallery was originally open and screened by Japanese style wooden blinds.

At the same time as Casa Vicens, Gaudí designed a villa known as El Capricho in Comillas on the Cantabrian coast near Santander. In this building the rooms are laid out more loosely and there is a more open relationship between interior and exterior, so reflecting a greater emphasis on the function and potential of light within the architectural structure. The decoration in Villa El Capricho shows great attention to detail and the entire building is covered with the same ceramic tiles, with sunflowers in marked relief, as those which decorate Casa Vicens.

20

21

The small fumoir (on these two pages) of Casa Vicens has a decidedly Islamic feel. One original and interestingly executed feature is a Moorish vault with stalactites from which hangs a lamp decorated with Arabic script, so combining natural and artificial light sources. Between the painted plaster stalactites forming stylised palm branches hang bunches of dates. The walls have a high dado in painted ceramic and papier mâché wallpaper.

24

In 1883 the cultivated industrialist and merchant Eusebio Güell bought an estate at Les Corts de Sarriá, now Avenida Pedralbes in Barcelona. He gave Gaudí responsibility for rebuilding the villa and designing the porter's lodge (facing page), cowsheds, stables and the wall marking the end of the estate. Surviving examples of Gaudí's work here include the splendid main gate (this page) as well as the porter's lodge, cowsheds and stable, built in the mudéjar *or Nazarene style.*

The mudéjar *influence is particularly evident in the brick and terracotta wall decoration made up of staggered circular elements. The large dining room and two upper rooms in the porter's lodge are covered with a spherical roof crowned by a lantern. To create the fantastic gate, with its enormous mythical dragon guarding the garden of the Hesperides, Gaudí used wrought iron, ingeniously combining traditional Catalan craftsmanship with wire mesh.*

In the pavilions of Finca Güell, the individual elements where Gaudí tends to shake off the Mudéjar influence are more pleasing than the work as a whole. Personal, distinctive touches include the lanterns on the porter's lodge (detail, below left) and the spacious lantern which stands on top of the large hyperboloid cupola of the stables (facing page). These are covered with multi-coloured ceramic consisting of pieces of tile arranged in lively geometric patterns.

Tile fragments were much more suited to covering Gaudí's curved surfaces than whole tiles. Because of this he is credited with inventing a new type of mosaic. The antimonial decoration on top of the gatepost (above right) represents an orange tree, symbol of the garden of the Hesperides. The pavilions of Finca Güell showed how the young Gaudí was able to interpret historical styles with great freedom, and mark his first use of parabolic arches and vaults.

In 1886 Gaudí was commissioned to build a town house for Eusebio Güell. The final plan resulted in a house that aroused much discussion at the time because it was so different from other houses in the city. Palacio Güell was in fact Gaudí's first completely independent work. For the first time he had to face the problem of space and resolved it in an original manner that transcends any considerations of style. Reworked Byzantine and Moorish architectural features are, however, present - together with formal solutions which anticipate

Art Nouveau. The most interesting exterior features include two catenary arches closed, for the first time in Barcelona, not by a wooden door but by wrought iron gates letting in light. Two sets of parabolic arch windows make up a front arcade that acts as a filter between interior and exterior. From the entrance hall (opposite), where the structure is no longer masked by decoration as in Gaudí's first works, stairs lead up to the drawing room on the first floor (below).

Gaudí's original sense of space is fully apparent inside Palacio Güell where the multi-story structure is, as it were, cancelled out by the central hall around which the other rooms are arranged. The great hall (this page), topped with a parabolic cupola, rises up through the three floors of the building. The cupola, rests on parabolic arches and is surmounted by another cupola topped by a spire. The room is lit from above through holes in the roof and four dormer windows at the sides.

The parabolic arches in the front arcade of the central hall of Palacio Güell stand on marble columns with hyperboloid capitals (facing page). The ceiling is a Gaudían interpretation of Moorish architecture. The room was used as a concert hall, reception room and chapel. The central spire emerging from the roof terrace is surrounded by eighteen chimney pots (detail below), which are totally different from one another in shape and decoration and create a fantastic, imaginative landscape.

The Colegio Teresiano was begun in September 1888, working to a plan designed by an unknown architect. Gaudí was commissioned to complete the work in March the following year. Since the building was already built to first floor level, he could not alter the layout and had to be content with changing only the outside. He gave this an austere appearance reminiscent of his work on the Neo-gothic Bishop's Palace of Astorga in Castille. In the Colegio the materials, bare brickwork and crushed stone, are treated with Gaudí's customary, highly sensitive touch.

The exterior is broken up into a rhythmic series of tall windows with false arches in bare brick. The terraced roof is crenellated with corner turrets featuring twisted columns bearing the shield of the Carmelite Order, and a red cross with four arms on top (this page). The front and rear of the building are spanned by projecting central tribunes with terracotta grills (facing page) in triangular patterns reminiscent of Finca Güell.

One very eye-catching feature of the Colegio Teresiano is its entrance hall, made up of parabolic arches and a very fine wrought iron gate (facing page). The cloistered austerity of the building's interior fits in perfectly with the exterior. It is remarkable for the simplicity of its spatial organisation and the absence of bright colours and other decorative features so abundant in Gaudí's early work. The most interesting areas of the building are a courtyard surrounded by a corridor of delicate, very closely spaced parabolic arches, and the first floor corridor, also made up of parabolic arches (this page). This clearly reflects an extremely personal and original interpretation of Gothic themes which differs markedly from any other contemporary revivalist form.

The Colegio Teresiano was completed in 1889. Although subsequently extended without the help of Antoni Gaudí, it nevertheless remains, despite the lack of financial backing, the most interesting Gaudian building of its period.

The design for Casa Calvet is dated 29th March 1898. The building was completed in 1900, when Barcelona City Council awarded it a prize as the best building of the year. The fine sandstone façade displays Baroque influences in the coping with two curves that tops the roof terrace, the sculpted decoration on the veranda over the main entrance (below) resting on a corbel bearing the owner's initials and in the presence of a cypress, the symbol of hospitality - quite apart from the elaborately ornamented ironwork of the three-lobed balconies.

Baroque influences and Modernist trends are very apparent in the entrance hall and lift well (facing page). These are profusely decorated with twisted columns and palmate capitals together with bent and wrought iron, wood and glass. The house's richly inventive rear façade is broken up with continuous glazed bands that alternate with balconies. Other features worthy of note include benches and seats in anatomical shapes, and hall furniture. These were designed by Gaudí and are now in the Gaudí Museum.

In 1895, Güell decided to construct a building with apartments, shops, wine cellars and a chapel for the staff of his wine-producing company in Garraf, near Sitges, on the rocky Mediterranean coast. The building is in local stone and brick and was finished at the beginning of this century. It still represents a splendid example of perfect integration with the adjacent ancient buildings. These include a medieval tower that Gaudí joined to the new buildings with a parabolic arch. Gaudí's colleague Francisco Berenguer Mestres

(1866-1914) played such a large rôle in directing work on the Güell Cantinas that he considered the building all his own work - despite the fact that this claim was quite without foundation. Facing page, a view of the Güell Cantinas with the adjacent porter's lodge and the main gateway with its fine iron gate of interwoven chains. Below, a detail of the upper part of the building occupied by the chapel, with parabolic arches, situated between the two great slopes of the roof.

In 1900, Gaudí was commissioned by Doñ *María Sagués, widow of Figueras,* to design a house surrounded by a garden in the outskirts of Barcelona in the Bellesguard estate. This contains the ruins of an ancient pavilion built by Martin I, King of Aragon, in 1409. After restoring part of the original wall left standing, Gaudí rerouted a road so that the ancient royal residence could be enclosed by the villa garden. In order to do this, he built a viaduct over the Belén river with sloping pillars to contain the thrust of the embankment instead

of the usual wall and projections (this page). Gaudí was to use this solution extensively in Parque Güell. The Bellesguard Villa (facing page) was designed entirely by Gaudí who directed the work on his own until 1909. After this date the task was taken over by Domingo Sugrañes, who collaborated with him on other projects. The building, completed in 1916, is in the Gothic style but reflects a highly individual interpretation.

Bellesguard is a square tower with an angular spire surmounted by the royal crown and Gaudí's distinctive trademark, a four-armed cross. The building is in terracotta and stone with delicately coloured faces in local stone and relief decorations made out of tiny stones and fragments of majolica ware. This type of decoration was achieved by placing the material in a mould and then adding mortar. The stone then remained on the surface when the mould was overturned. On this page: the entrance and part of the façade.

White is the dominant colour inside the Bellesguard tower and the forms of the arches, banisters (this page) and ceilings are very fluid, rounded and well-lit. The large relief window on the staircase (below) contains a large stained glass star that represents the planet Venus, symbol of love, in memory of the marriage between Martin the Humanist and Margaret of Prades celebrated in Bellesguard in 1409.

One of the most interesting
rooms in the Bellesguard
tower is the strange mansard
standing two floors high
(shown here). It consists of
slender terracotta columns
that expand into a mushroom-
shaped capital and very light
ceramic entablature. This is
the starting point for lobed
arches which extend from the
vault like palm leaves and
divide the vault, which
consists of a network of bricks
arranged in triangular shapes,
into sections.
The architect Rubió claims
that it is impossible to see
how some of the structures at
Bellesguard manage to stay
up. Gaudí's special solutions
defy the normal rules of
construction engineering.
Another distinctive feature of
the building is its roof, shaped
like a truncated pyramid.
This is broken up by jutting
skylights and encircling steps
that lead to the upper part of
the building. The ribbed
arches in the dormitories are
also of great interest. Villa
Bellesguard is still a private
residence.

In about 1900 Eusebio Güell had the idea of creating a garden city in Barcelona and set aside an estate on the outskirts of the city for this purpose. Gaudí transformed this uneven piece of land into one of his most fantastic creations. The work lasted several years and during this time roads were built and sixty plots of land set aside for houses with gardens. The undertaking was an economic failure and abandoned in 1914. The land was made into a public park in 1922.

One of the structures Gaudí created for the Parque Güell was the double stairway shown opposite. At the top of this is a vast colonnade with eighty-six Doric columns. These are hollow inside and convey rainwater from the terrace above them to a tank. From here, water is fed to the two fountains on the stairway. One of these is decorated with an iguana (above) and the other with the Shield of Catalonia and a serpent's head. Both are covered with multi-coloured tiles.

The main entrance to Parque Güell is overlooked by the porter's lodge (facing page). This stone building is decorated with majolica ware and culminates in a tower with a four-armed cross on top. The wrought-iron gate (below), with its palm leaf design, comes from Casa Vicens. The park contains only two buildings apart from the entrance pavilions. One was built as a "model" (Gaudí lived in it for a long time and it is now a museum) and the other was owned by one of Gaudí's friends, the only person to buy a plot of land.

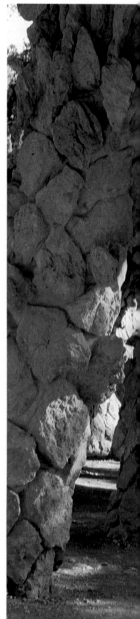

54

The main roads in Parque Güell are supported by arcades or run on viaducts held up by sloping columns, each of which differs in the design of the vault and shape of the column itself. Similar to grottoes in appearance, these arcades also act as covered walkways and offer protection against the sun or rain (below). The columns shown on the facing page are purely ornamental and topped with flower pots. This represents an important example of the way Gaudí blended architectural and natural forms.

In 1904, Gaudí was responsible for partly refurbishing Casa Batlló in Paseo de Gracia. He reorganised the inside of the first floor, restructured the rear façade and remodelled the main façade, decorating it with a strange dinosaur-like ceramic shape, and extended the inner courtyard. The very fine continuous modelling on the main façade produces a chiaroscuro effect that is subtle at the bottom and becomes gradually more pronounced higher up.

In Casa Batlló, as in his later Casa Milà, Gaudí was mainly inspired by natural motifs reminiscent of human and animal forms freely remodelling them with surreal results. The fine private staircase (facing page) was carved by hand, while the ceramic fireplace (above) in the entrance to the first floor apartment, as well as many other decorative features, display forms characteristic of magic Surrealism. When Casa Batlló is lit up by the morning sun, it looks like a lake of water-lilies in a Monet painting.

A round tower in Casa Batlló contains a spiral staircase leading to the mansard (below) with its roof of ribbed parabolic arches of different heights. The ridge of the shining, scale-covered roof is decorated with large ceramic beads that call to mind the backbone of a dinosaur. The tower ends in a bulbous form crowned with a four-armed cross (facing page, above). The helicoidal chimney stacks are surmounted with pyramid-shaped pots with spheres on top and treated as a group rather than as individual elements (facing page, below).

The Casa Milà (facing page) is situated on the corner of the elegant Paseo de Gracia in Barcelona. It was begun in 1906 and completed in 1910. This outstanding work was Gaudí's last secular building. It consists of a basement, five floors - all different from one another - and a penthouse. The very simple structure is made of stone, terracotta or iron pillars, and metal beams. The only walls are those around the perimeter. The inner space is divided into rooms by means of light partitions that enclose polygonal, often asymmetric spaces. The wavy,

façade extends horizontally and is made in rough stone to resemble an underwater reef. This has earned Casa Milà the popular name of "La Pedrera", which means "the stone quarry". The façade is set off by the dynamic wrought-iron work on the balconies, each one of them different. The design of the main entrance (this page) is inspired by forms occurring in nature. The façade is attached to the building's structure with concealed iron beams.

Facing page, entrance hall and staircase of Casa Milà. The ceiling on
the ground floor of this extraordinary building is supported by pillars.
The stair well, lit from the central courtyard, has a glass roof and is
adorned with jardinieres which also have the effect of enhancing the
wall looking out onto the courtyard. On this page, the ceilings of the
exhibition hall. The plaster ceiling in Casa Milà display relief patterns
inspired by animal and plant morphology - and each one is different.

Gaudí's visionary imagination really takes off in the great chimney and ventilation stacks which crowd the roof terrace of Casa Milà (this page). They look like people, monsters or warriors from some kind of surrealist vision. They were not designed as anthropomorphic figures, though, but based solely on geometrical shapes: variations on paraboloid, helicoid and hyperboloid themes. Gaudí chose neutral colours for these evocative monumental plastic forms.

In 1891 Eusebio Güell decided to extend his textile manufacturing business. He therefore moved his factory to Barcelona, to Santa Coloma de Cervelló where he also set up an estate for his workers. This consisted of 150 houses with shops and utilities. The work was commissioned from Gaudí but built mainly by Berenguer, although Gaudí took sole responsibility for the church on Colonia Güell. This was designed in about 1898 but begun only ten years later and never completed. Work was stopped when Güell died in 1918.

Only the crypt was completed, in 1915 (facing page). The building is made out of charred and broken bricks, basalt rock and black volcanic stone in colours that blended in perfectly with the surrounding environment - the brown tones of undergrowth and tree trunks. Similarly, the windows (below) are decorated with green ceramic tiles reminiscent of leaves, and the top of the building is covered with blue and white majolica ware so that it merges with the sky. If the building had been completed according to plan, golden spires would have been added to simulate the rays of the sun.

The crypt of the Santa Coloma estate contains two sets of pillars (four central pillars in grey basalt and ten brick pillars round the outside) that are raked at different angles in different directions. This unusual structure obviously presented problems of balance that were resolved only by means of a long preliminary study based on exclusively empirical principles. Gaudí devised a mechanism of sliding hoists in his workshop. He attached weights to the pulleys to measure the forces pulling on the structure. He then turned the model upside down so that the pulling forces became pushing forces proportional to those acting on the actual structure. The roof to the crypt is flat, made out of bricks and divided up by large, fanned ribs that produce a lively decorative effect while also supporting the church above. The brightly-coloured stained glass windows were designed by Gaudí, who took care of every detail including the pews and the font.

The Sagrada Familia

The Church of the Sagrada Familia is Gaudí's magnum opus
and incorporates all the features for which he is famous. He
began work on it on 3rd November 1883, taking over from
Francisco de Paula who had built only part of the crypt.
Gaudí then devoted himself to the task of building this
grandiose monument for the next forty-three years. From
1914 to 1926, the year he died, he worked on nothing else and
even lived in a little room on the building site so he would
never have to leave it. He saw the building as a work of
atonement and its importance lay more in its construction
than its completion. He calculated that it would take two
hundred years to finish and for this reason made a model to
crystallize the religious vision that inspired him and left future
generations of architects to carry on his work using the
techniques they considered most appropriate. According to
the plan, the church was laid out in the form of a Latin cross
with five naves, and a transept with a nave and two aisles. He
designed the exterior of the church with three façades, each
dominated by four high towers to symbolise the twelve
apostles. A central tower above the transept, surrounded by
four other towers, was designed to represent Christ and the
four Evangelists. Seven chapels opened off the presbytery that
led into the central chapel dedicated to Our Lady of the
Assumption. At the opposite end of the church a baptismal
chapel and a confessional chapel were to have flanked the main
entrance. The nave was to have been a mass of columns, quite
unlike a Gothic cathedral. Gaudí balanced out the system of
forces at work within the structure of his building preventing
a need for external elements such as rampant arches (he called
them "crutches"). He did this by bending the columns at an
angle equal to the resultant of the dynamic forces, using the
technique he developed for the crypt in Colonia Güell. Gaudí
succeeded in completing only the crypt nd most of the
Nativity Façade. Façing page, a section of this facade seen
from inside.

This page, a decorative detail on the Gateway of the Passion designed by Gaudí for the east transept in 1917 but not constructed until 1956. Following the destruction of most of the plans (during a fire in 1936), work on the Sagrada Familia was halted until a new model could be built. One of Gaudí's pupils, Quintana, was appointed to supervise the work. He had already been responsible for completing the Nativity Façade following Gaudí's death.

Opposite the Passion Façade, Gaudí designed the Nativity Façade (facing page) for the east transept. Three doors designed to represent Faith, Hope and Charity are set into the front. These are all richly decorated with statues and sculptures of great symbological complexity. Of the four towers dedicated to the Apostles Barnabas, Simon, Jude and Matthew, only the first was built by Gaudí and intended to serve as a model for the others. The third, main façade was dedicated to Glory.

Facing page, the Gateway of Charity in the Nativity Façade. Below, detail showing the Holy Family. Gaudí used ordinary people, often met by chance, as models for his biblical figures. He photographed them in front of a system of mirrors in order to obtain their image from different vantage points. He then made a plaster model that he fixed to the façade in order to take stock of its position and make any changes necessary to correct any visual distortion caused by distance. Only then did he make the statue in stone.

Index